WORDS

by **Selma Lola Chambers**
illustrated by **Louis Cary**

A GOLDEN BOOK • NEW YORK

Western Publishing Company, Inc., Racine, Wisconsin 53404

INTRODUCTION

It is fascinating for very young children to associate a word with its pictorial representation.

In The Little Golden Book of WORDS, each small picture represents a specific word. The pictures are arranged in groups — The Family, Things That Grow, Things That Go, Numbers, and so forth. Children will enjoy finding pictures of familiar objects and activities.

The Little Golden Book of WORDS is intended for use by children who are just learning to read. They will soon begin to associate the written symbols with the pictures.

This book offers many opportunities for games of word recognition and spelling. If left to the spontaneous use of young children, it is likely to lead to a great variety of activities.

The Family

grandfather

mother

father

grandmother

brother

baby

sister

People

he   she

man   woman

children

they

girl

boy

More People

postman

neighbor

fireman

policewoman

teacher

ice-cream man

friends

Colors

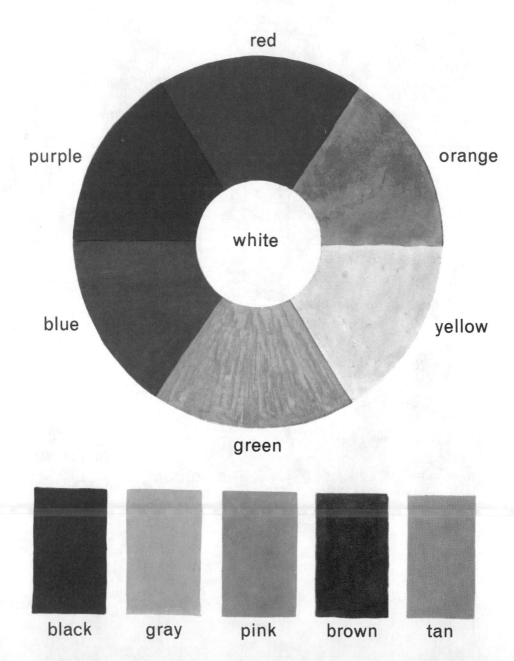

violet

red

yellow

black

orange

blue

brown

green

pink

gray

white

Things to Play With

horn

balloon

sled

jump rope

truck

drum

teddy bear

kite

wagon

doll   ball

puzzle

train

tricycle

blocks

marbles   roller skates

swing

slide

seesaw

dog

Clothes

earmuffs

skirt

shirt

pajamas

rubbers

snowsuit

mittens

boots

suit

socks

slippers

overalls

dress

hat

coat

shoes

underwear

sweater

pants

gloves

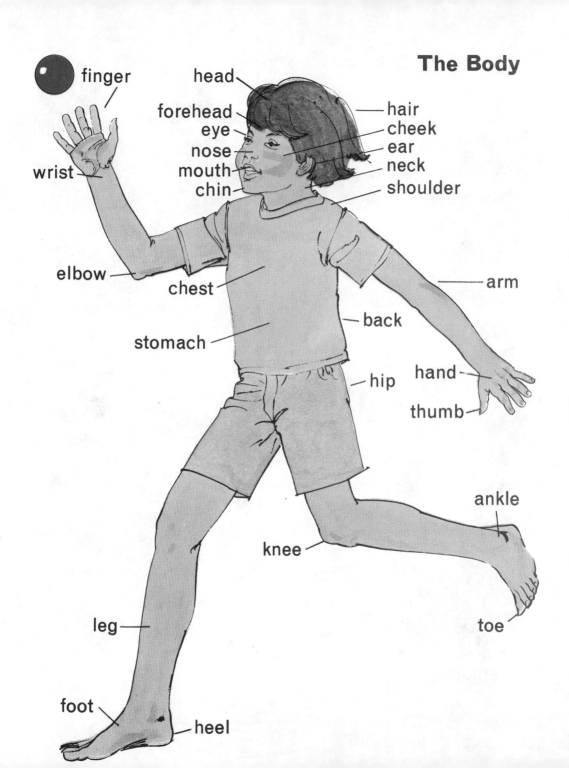

The Body

finger
head
forehead
eye
nose
mouth
chin
wrist
hair
cheek
ear
neck
shoulder
elbow
arm
chest
back
stomach
hip
hand
thumb
ankle
knee
leg
toe
foot
heel

Things to Eat

eggs

carrot

apple

milk

cake

orange

cheese

potato

jelly

corn

celery

tomato

grapefruit

peach

candy

banana

cookies

meat

lettuce

bread and butter

grapes

pear

ice cream

pancakes

Things That Grow

tree

strawberry

flower

bush

weed

corn

fern

vine

tree

grass

Things We Do

jump

work

write

dance

swing

build

run

walk

draw

blow

swim

read

crawl

sleep

eat

Things We Use

spoon

glass

dishes

paper

pan

broom

knife

fork

table

chair

clock

crayons

iron

hairbrush

comb

pencil

toothbrush

soap

radio

paintbrush

book

telephone

paints

box

television

towel

Things That Go

rocket

airplane

tractor

taxi

car

truck

trailer truck

motorboat

helicopter

fire engine

bus

train

steamship

Places to Go

home

movies

beach

park

school

country

yard

museum

city

store

friend's house

zoo

church

Zoo Animals

monkey

bear

fox

giraffe

deer

lion

elephant

turtle

snake

hippopotamus

Farm Animals

goat

horse

pig

sheep

cat

cow

dog

owl

Birds

chicken

robin

duck

parrot

pigeon

turkey

crow

sparrow

eagle

canary

Word Helpers

to the store

from the store

stop

go

in the house

out of the house

over the fence

under the fence

empty

full

up the stairs

down the stairs

socks on

socks off

raining

not raining

before
the haircut

after the haircut

many fish

few fish

old shoes

new shoes

Shapes and Sizes

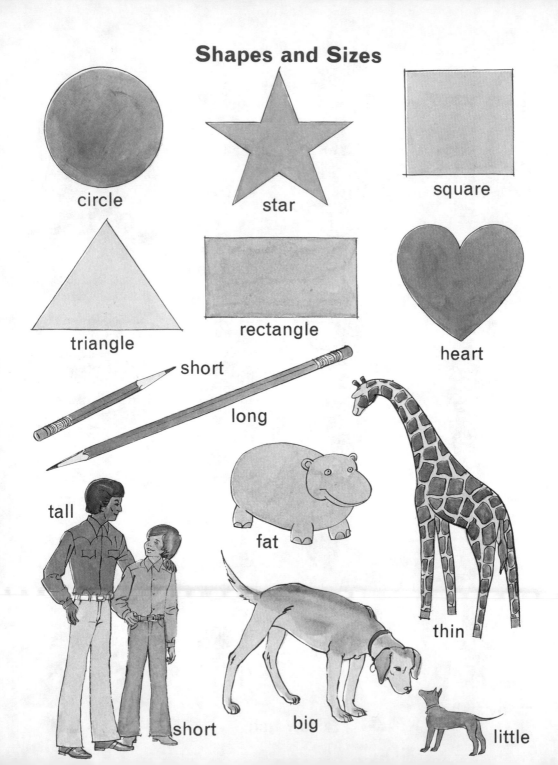

circle

star

square

triangle

rectangle

heart

short

long

tall

fat

thin

short

big

little

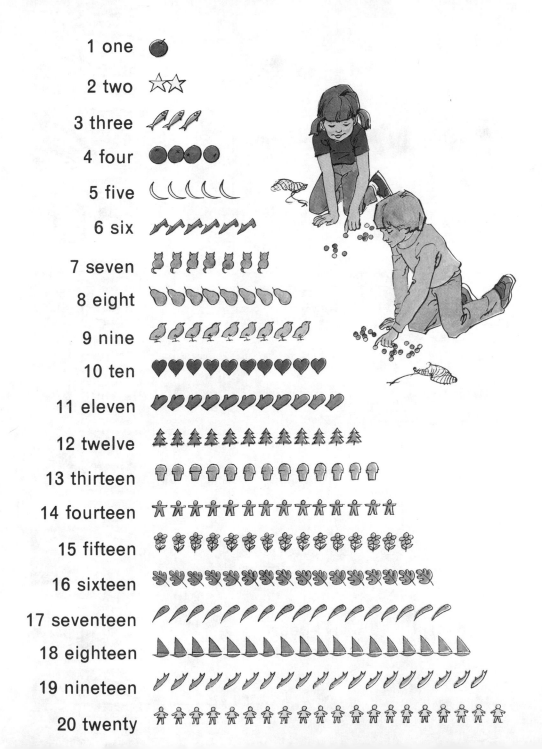

1 one

2 two

3 three

4 four

5 five

6 six

7 seven

8 eight

9 nine

10 ten

11 eleven

12 twelve

13 thirteen

14 fourteen

15 fifteen

16 sixteen

17 seventeen

18 eighteen

19 nineteen

20 twenty

The Alphabet

I igloo

A apple

B box

C cat

D dog

E elephant

F fish

G goat

H hat

J jelly

K kite

L lion

M mittens

N nest

O octopus

P pear

Q queen

R rabbit

S seal

T table

U umbrella

V valentine

W wagon

X X ray

Y yarn

Z zebra